Pittsburghese

Pittsburghese

POEMS BY **ROBERT GIBB**

Wheelbarrow Books ▪ *East Lansing, Michigan*

♾ The paper used in this publication meets the minimum requirements of ANSI/NISO Z39.48-1992 (R 1997) (Permanence of Paper).

Wheelbarrow Books
Michigan State University Press
East Lansing, Michigan 48823-5245

LIBRARY OF CONGRESS CATALOGING-IN-PUBLICATION DATA
Names: Gibb, Robert, 1946– author.
Title: Pittsburghese : poems / by Robert Gibb.
Description: First edition. | East Lansing, Michigan : Wheelbarrow Books, [2023]
Identifiers: LCCN 2023021611 | ISBN 9781611864878 (paper) |
ISBN 9781609177577 (PDF) | ISBN 9781628955200 (ePub)
Subjects: LCSH: Pittsburgh (Pa.)—Poetry. | LCGFT: Poetry.
Classification: LCC PS3557.I139 P58 2023 | DDC 811/.54—dc23/eng/20230518
LC record available at https://lccn.loc.gov/2023021611

Cover design by Erin Kirk
Cover art is Pittsburgh Steel Company, Monessen Works, Donner Avenue,
Monessen, Westmoreland County, PA, 1991, photograph by Jet Lowe.

Visit Michigan State University Press at *www.msupress.org*

With the publication of Robert Gibb's *Pittsburghese*, the Residential College in the Arts and Humanities (RCAH) Center for Poetry at Michigan State University offers its thirteenth book in our Wheelbarrow Books Poetry Series. Clearly, we pay homage to William Carlos Williams and his iconic poem, "The Red Wheelbarrow." Readers will remember the poem begins "so much depends upon" that red wheelbarrow. In our country today with significant issues of climate change, inflation, covid variants, cultural fracture, and political unrest, many people would say their lives do not depend upon poetry. Far from it. Ezra Pound told us, however, that "poetry is news that stays news." This is not "fake news," or yesterday's news, or old news. Good poems have immediacy, present us with specific people in specific situations not unlike our own, and, most of all, poems tell us the truth. "The first function of poetry is to tell the truth," June Jordan reminds us, "to learn how to do that, to find out what you really feel and what you really think."

The list of contemporary elegies, and elegies in general, is long and varied by subject, and ranges from small poems like Theodore Roethke's "Elegy for Jane, My Student Thrown by a Horse," to Edward Hirsch's book length *Gabriel* or bell hooks's *appalachian elegy*. In the first three sentences of Elizabeth Alexander's poem, "Fortune," she writes, "My father is dead. He died of arteriosclerosis, not enough oxygen in his blood. He never felt full-fledged sick, but he was always nauseous, or dizzy. Out of sorts."

In *Pittsburghese*, Robert Gibb has given us an elegy for place, the Pittsburgh area late in the twentieth century, and specifically Homestead, about eleven miles southeast of Pittsburgh, which in 1900 had a population 12,554 people, of whom some 7,000 were employed in the steel plants. By 1980, it had become difficult to obtain employment at the Homestead Steel Works, which was not producing much steel at that time. In 1986, the mill closed. The Homestead Works was demolished in the early 1990s, replaced in 1999 by the Waterfront shopping mall. As a direct result of the loss of mill employment, the number of people living in Homestead dwindled. By the time of the 2010 census, the borough population was 3,165 (The Pittsburgh Survey). Though these poems are set in and near Pittsburgh, they could take place in any mill town or industrial city in Pennsylvania, Ohio, West Virginia, or Kentucky. This was a place with not enough oxygen in its blood, its people nauseous, dizzy, and out of sorts.

The story of Pittsburgh and its people is in the hands of a good storyteller. Through Gibb's striking images and specific details, we find we are living and working along with the people in town. Several of his poems are based on photographs taken over the years, and in one titled, "*Home Scrap Project: Unemployed Steel Worker, 1987–1988*," he writes,

> Each testament a part of the portraiture,
> Each background story fronted
> In its own signature scrawl.

One of those being "*loss of wife & family, loss of friends, / loss of self-respect & esteem.*" In a poem based on the painting, "*Homestead*, ca. 1929. Oil on Canvas," Gibb talks of the "Detail-driven landscapes" of John Kane (1860–1934), "Taking in the features / Of the 'industrial sublime.'" That was then. "The Etymologies of Rust" is now.

But the poems in *Pittsburghese* are not all about all rust and ruin. There is music in these poems, not just the poems on "The Immanence of 78s" or "On the Removal of the Stephen Foster Statue from Schenley Plaza in Pittsburgh" or The Blind Boys of Alabama or the Crystals and Ronettes, but music in Gibb's precise choice of words and the cadence of language throughout the poems. In "The Age of Innocence," the poem closes with

> I catch the flash
> Of handshakes, their elaborate dance,
>
> The few girls huddled by the cars,
> Streetlights above them and the first wheeling stars.

There is music also in memory, and we find it in such poems as "Park Elementary," "Bildungsroman," "The Pittsburgh Athletic Association," and "Phone Booths," where you were

> Snugged in, out of earshot, and about to have your say.
> Landlines, sea-floor cables, creosoted poles—

You were umbilical with all of it.
Now the thick world's housed in a cloud.

Thomas Wolfe told us, "You can't go home again," but I would argue that, in poems and in memory, you can. An elementary school or a phone booth, a steel mill or a worker's orange helmet, in reading these fine poems, I returned to my childhood near Charleston, West Virginia, a city of chemical plants lining the Kanawha River, many of which are now defunct or greatly reduced in size, and to my DuPont worker father who feared the coming of automation. Robert Gibb has captured a time in American history with the specificity of his places, events, and people. As I read the stories rising from his memory, my own did, too, reminding me of one of the great gifts of poetry: connections to others and to the larger world.

As our number of Wheelbarrow Books increases, we hope that our audience increases also. Help us spread the word. In the beginning was the word, we're told, and the word became the poem. So much depends upon the collaboration of reader, writer, and poem, the intimate ways we come to know one another.

—ANITA SKEEN, *Wheelbarrow Books Series Editor*

Pittsburghese is the language spoken in the pages of this poet's singular concoction, a mix of keen musicality and uncommon sagacity that wound itself purposely and sinuously through my imagination like the twisty hills and bridges of its hometown. I'm sitting in a cab listening to the driver tour me through what lies beneath the voices of the Blind Boys of Alabama, I'm perched in the bar with the voices fresh from the blast furnaces, glowering about the sweat of each shift, I'm nodding with the poet at the jukebox that diphones all our sounds from Stephen Foster to Ray Charles and beyond. In the tradition of learning the sacred, secret loves of a burnished and bellowed metropolis, this poet's voice masterfully testifies to neighborhoods and lives doused in enough heat to melt, but then forged in enough wry and heartbusted love to craft the wiry steel of these poems.

—TYEHIMBA JESS

for Maggie & Matthew

CONTENTS

Pittsburghese . . . a dialect of American English
—Wikipedia

A local habitation and a name
—*A Midsummer Night's Dream*

I

The Pittsburgh Athletic Association

where Pittsburgh's elites began gathering
in the early 1900s to socialize and enjoy
state-of-the-art athletic facilities
—*Pittsburgh Post-Gazette*

That ornate, stone, Italianate building
With its tiered and pillared façade
Was the closest I ever got to posh,
My cousin's family my ticket of admission.
A broad, softly lit lobby islanded with
Round settees. The white-tiled locker room
We changed in, its aging Black attendant
Stationed beside his stack of towels.
Amenities the term they used to cover that.
A far cry from our dinged-up gym
In its wing of the Homestead Library—
One of the ones Carnegie built, spending
A fraction of the fortune he'd made
Off the backs of men like my grandfather.
The term for which is still *philanthropist*.
A stack of freshly laundered towels,
Tips scattered in the bowl beside it.
Those Saturdays I spent in Oakland,
Coming of age, I had the great buildings
For my backdrop, the sidewalks
Made exotic by interns wearing scrubs
And women their saffron-colored saris.
Had the contingent at the trolley stop,
Following an afternoon ballgame.
This morning I read in the *Post-Gazette*
That the P.A.A. will be auctioning off
Its contents at a sheriff's sale, furniture

3

Included, and the lobby paintings
I'd pause before—horses posed in profile,
And those lush green landscapes
The decades had dusked with gold.
Hardly the cautery of light I watched
Burning nightly above the slag heaps.
It was trust-funded William F. Buckley
Who said proximity to a public library
Was one of the perks of the urban poor,
Sounding like the Carnegie who coined
The "morality of self-improvement."
His philanthropy a form of self-esteem,
Though others were beggared by the cost.

Deskulling the Slag Pots

I.

We'd see them in the railyard,
Narrow-gauged and waiting
To be topped off with that cargo
Tapped from the blast furnaces:
Magma to be freighted out
  Along the spine of the hill
To where the pots were tipped,
  Their guttering eruptions spilled
From the horizon's line of fire—
Auroras of white-hot scoria
That we'd see nightly, storming
Down the side of the sky.

II.

Slag that sat in the pots too long
Hardened into the plugged
And cindery, dust-caked skulls
We had to shuck and trepan,
The crane's pile-driver chisel
  Dropped to rupture the crusts,
Disgorging the molten dross
  Of oxides in a sudden gush.
A core that matched the planet's,
It always seemed, or mimicked
The cosmic egg at the Big Bang
Exploding its fiery yolk.

Home Scrap Project: Unemployed Steel Worker, 1987–1988

photographs by Ramon Elouza

A row of close-cropped, full-color headshots—
His eye-level lineup stares out at us
From behind lines of writing,

well I lost my job my wife and about to lose
my home because of the shut down

Each testament a part of the portraiture,
Each background story fronted
In its own signature scrawl.

no one wants to hire me because I am a steel worker
made too much money working at the mill

It must have felt like they were filling out
Still one more requisite form
To be filed away and forgotten.

my spouse has supported the household since
my layoff & ran out of unemployment funds

The harshness of the colors, part of the portraits
As well, as if they'd been developed
In some brownfield seep,

loss of wife & family, loss of friends,
loss of self-respect & esteem

Some acidic bath in which their battered stares
First surfaced—socketed in bone—
Each pigmented iris, pupil's black hole.

Musicology

I.

When The Blind Boys of Alabama paired the lyrics
Of "Amazing Grace" with the dirge-like melody
Of "House of the Rising Sun," they knew what
They were doing, bringing blues back into the fold,
The young girl's ruin into the sanctified strains
Of the gospel tradition, bridging divisions
That bedeviled singers for most of the past century.

"Was blind and now I see" setting the testifying
Standard for us all. Unless that melody was their way
Of conceding that the soul is fused to the flesh
So completely its music can't be other than the blues,
The gutbucket sacraments of sex and death
The passions of that play. The soul at the crossroads.
The soul with its mojo hands and black cat bones.

In Georgia Turner's version, "Rising Sun Blues,"
What the blind-no-more singer clearly sees
Is that hope's a form of despair she can't afford
Any longer, except for the baby sister she asks
The listener to warn—"Never do what I have done"—
As if that's all she wants from life, or has any right
To expect, seeing how her race is almost run.

7

II.

A house like the ones in the zodiac, the rising sun
Its sign. The first time I heard it—opening notes
And knowing vocal, the lush surge of chords
From the keyboard—the Animals' version electrified
The air inside the car. The first hit to cross over
From the acoustic folk-revival rolls, its sense
Of transgression and penance was electric as well.

I'd been driving around the streets of Homestead,
Darkness coming on, fires from the mills on the river,
The old sporting houses still going strong
In that Storyville along the tracks at Sixth Avenue.
A world the song seemed to speak of, clear back
To my grandfather's day, rerouted now through
Birmingham on the waves of the British Invasion.

What was new about the song was how much older
It seemed, and haunted, how much closer
It cleaved to the bone. "Sin and misery" went
The lament, backed by those folk-blues' licks.
Barely a year had passed since the firebombing
Of the Baptist Church in Birmingham, Alabama.
Four young girls dead, the fire next time nearly here.

Impulse!

Those blaze-orange and jet-black logos
Tagging their jackets in the record bins
Caught your attention as intended,
A new world coming into view in 1960,
The year I entered high school, though
Coltrane's *Africa/Brass* was still another
School year away. Each new title—
Passin' Thru, Nights of Ballads & Blues—
Hinted of the vistas the stylus tracked
To 1964, when *Live at Birdland* broke
Over me like the heavens during a storm.
When the mode of the music changes,
Plato wrote, the walls of the city shake.
Commencement meant entering a world
Of turmoil at home (Freedom Summer
One of the stations of the decade's cross),
As well as in the false-flagged waters
Of the Gulf of Tonkin halfway across
The globe. Within a year I'd be working
At U.S. Steel, clearing scale from slabs
Plunged into a furnace, attending to
The engines of the cold war economy.
FM radio coming into its own, I'd stay up
Nights, dialed-in to the incandescence
That lit up my room, whole album sides
At times. *Fire Music* and *Dear John C.*
How the state coveted the adolescent
Male body it needed to feed its ranks.
Agent, not blaze, the name of that orange.
Music the blaze marks we followed.
Impressions. Crescent. A Love Supreme.
Each record better than the one before,

Years when such bounty was boundless.
(Ragas in the Village Vanguard,
Sheets of sound in "Eight Miles High.")
Coltrane died when I was in boot camp,
Shorn and lost and uniformed,
Conscript for the coming apocalypse.

Last Round: For Rufus Harley

> O Bag-pipe thou didst re-assert thy sway
> —Keats

Decked out on the cover of *Scotch & Soul*

In regalia's kilt and cap, he's cradling
The bagpipes in the crook of an arm,

Lathe-turned chanter and drones against

His left shoulder—the full complement
Of trappings for that plaid skirling haggis

Coltrane once asked to take lessons on.

*

I'd put it on the turntable late at night,

Empties scattered about, trying to align
My friends with those soulful anthems

For what was most adamant and wild.

Keats found it in Burns, visiting his grave
And birthplace, the "sea-shore iron scurf"

He stood before later, taking it all in.

Homestead, *ca. 1929. Oil on Canvas*

John Kane, 1860–1934

Bird's-eye, as in mid-flight, midair
    And slightly upriver,
.   The bridge in the foreground
And its watered-down reflection
    Parallel to the picture plane.
        The sky fluffed up with clouds.
Not quite Giotto's God's-eye view
    In which the world gets seen
        From all sides. Homestead
Is crowded rows of houses,
    Steel mills billowing
        Identical plumes of smoke,
Bent level toward the horizon—
    One of his vernacular,
        Detail-driven landscapes,
Description like composition
    A way to lead the eye around it,
        Taking in the features
Of the "industrial sublime."
    Scumble and glaze came later.
        Here the world is local color,
The way he first applied it,
    Painting scenes on the sides
        Of boxcars during lunchbreaks
At work. A job he'd likely
    Thought of while brushing in
        The slow freights he's strung
Along either side of the river.

He's got its slurry just right,
And the massive scale
Of the open hearths, pikestaffs
Of the blast furnace chimneys.
1929. The economy
About to tank as if in another country.

Worker, Steel Mill

photograph by W. Eugene Smith, ca. 1955

Anonymous in those glare-filled goggles,

He's gauntleted and cassocked, garbed
To be garbed in fire, which forms a lake

On the floor behind him and fills the doors
Of the blast furnace stoves behind that—

Coke and pig iron being melted down,

Tapped out through the cinder notches,
The crucible mass charged to make steel.

Steps of that flaming dance Smith saw
As part of the mills' brutal music.

Because the earth's so much raw material

The weeks have been divided into shifts,
The days into work and what's left over.

Because the business cycle is relentless,
He works turns that follow the clock,

Punching in before pulleying his robes

Down from where he'd left them
Halfway to heaven in the ceiling's loft,

Then dressing to take his station again,
The clotted fires fissuring their troughs.

Because of the costs of production.

The Immanence of 78s

Thick, black, pressed-shellac disks,
Lipped, then grooved with spirals,
Annular with the "dead wax" bands
Smoothly moating the labels: *Black Patti*
With its peacock, *Paramount* its raptor,
Great wings mantling the planet.
Frangible and stiff, they're auraed
Like something discovered in a tomb,
Stashed among the necessities,
Their otherworldly voices exhumed.
Delta blues recorded in Memphis
And the upper Midwest,
"Race records" the marketing niche.
It took me decades to fully connect
With the music furrowed in them.
"Cypress Grove" and "Levee Camp."
My father's shelves were crammed
With jazz, LPs mostly, though
I found a copy of *Bluebird Blues*
Among them, the sampling of artists
That got me started—Ruby Glaze
And Hot Shot Willie, Lonnie Johnson
With Lil Hardin Armstrong on piano.
Decades to our tactile-starved age
Where the simple presence
Of the records is a treasure. *Gennett*
And *Champion*, their gothic fonts,
The *Broadways*' cloud-backed skylines.
Human consciousness, said Jung,
Finds its way into the things around us,
Giving them their resonance in time.
The way, pressed into these 78s,
Blues are fused to the common clay.

On the Removal of the Stephen Foster Statue
from Schenley Plaza in Pittsburgh

Who wouldn't throw shade on the past
When it's in blackface, given half a chance?
But what to make of this particular rebuke
To the father of our popular music
(And honored guest in the dissonance
Of Charles Ives), his songs a rich soil, wrote
Frederick Douglass, in which "sympathies
for the slave" flourished. His songs the near-
Alluvial source material for musicians like
Louis Armstrong. In 1900 Giuseppe Moretti
Sculpted his Foster in the act of composing
"Uncle Ned," manumitted below him,
Banjo on his knee. A sufficient enough whiff
Of minstrelsy to have led to the statue's
Removal, banishing in the bargain this
Enactment of the song. Now that the statue's
Been cancelled, how to point out that Foster
Was never the fount of its music, looking
About as downhome as an accountant,
Poorer for the contrast with the frailing Ned,
Camped closer to the provenant earth?
Still, our music's far from mutually exclusive
(The Child Ballads lurking in the blues),
The country playing catch-up as usual.
In 1957 Ray Charles shot right to the top
Of the pop charts with "Swanee River Rock,"
Having syncopated Foster's "Old Folks
at Home." I'd sooner anthem it any day
Than "The Star Spangled Banner," even with
Those slave-hunting hosannas removed.

II

The Etymologies of Rust

I.

From the OE. *rúst* and the kinship of cognates,
Dutch and Germanic, plus ON.

II.

The slow, remorseless kind of oxidation.
The effacing effects of time.

III.

Rust & mohða in the Lindisfarne Gospel, ca. 950 AD.

IV.

Any deteriorating or impairing effect.
Any uredinous fungus.
Cankers like corrosion on idled iron.

V.

Rust & mohða because the moth is dust already,
Powdery with the pigments of its wings.

VI.

Red, orange, or tawny. The ferrous of flakes.
Stiff burrs on the furnaces in the rust belt.

VII.

Garments, said the psalmist, *fretted by the moth.*

Pittsburghese

Take *jaggers*, for instance,
Which here is vernacular for brambles,
Derived from the dialect *jag (v.)*—

"To prick with something sharp,
as with a spur or thorn."

Something to kick against
At your own risk, according to
The hand-me-down proverb.

They'd snatch you if you passed
Too closely or distracted,

An argument that made its points
All at once, though you'd need
To engage them one by one,

Gingerly lifting the thorns away
From the snag of perforations.

You'd tweeze out any jagger tips
That had splintered beneath your skin.
The name itself still sticks.

The Play of Memory in Childhood Spaces

CHAPEL

Twenty-two splinters from the True Cross
We were told, plus bones
From all twelve apostles.
Miraculous scraps of fabric as well.
And skulls in boxes.
"You have this word? Alcove?"
The *In Bruges* gun-thug asks in passing.
In Pittsburgh, on our class trip
To St. Anthony's Chapel,
We had "reliquary," but only as a word,
Till we were face to face
With those disinterred articles of faith.

23

COAL CELLAR

Up at street-level, at the top of the wall
In the basement's musty little room:
A cast-iron hatch, its hinges rusted shut,
Though I could clearly hear
The rumbling chute that day in school
As the teacher was reading to us—
"Load on load of apples coming in"—
Could see as in a dream of my own
How they glowed like coals in their bin,
Scenting the whole house above them.

BELVEDERE

Crow's-nest, dovecot, attic aerie—
The cupola I liked to imagine miter-boxed
And snugged about me, looking out
From a roost in the sky. Treetops
And chimneys. My head in the clouds
Now for real, ladder pulled up behind me,
Feet runged on the latched trapdoor.

COAT CLOSET

My first visit to my cousin's new address
In Providence. No sooner was I through
The door than I found another, hidden one
In the back wall of their front closet
And opened it upon another home entirely,
Another family staring up at me
From around their kitchen table, freezing me
In my tracks, and another of those moments
When I found myself alone in a world
Where the wrong door opened or closed.

NATALIE VAYDA'S BASEMENT

The house just one of our haunts
Who'd bivouacked in basements
Filled with old stoves and laundry tubs,
Shelves of pig's feet belled in brine
Like jars of dusky chum—
The past a memory palace after all,
Cached with its *phantasms*.

Phone Booths

Back before the private life went public, like shares,
They were a fixture of it, the cabinet kind
You'd find sentinel or all in a line
With their seats and shelves and pleated doors,
The lights coming on when they closed.
You sat in a closet the size of the confessional,
Dropping coins through their slots,
The clang of change tripping the circuitry open.
The dials were like the clocks back then,
Circumferenced with numbers, the phones black-
Boxed to walls on which clumsy glyphs
And messages were scrawled. So there you were,
Snugged in, out of earshot, and about to have your say.
Landlines, sea-floor cables, creosoted poles—
You were umbilical with all of it.
Now the thick world's housed in a cloud.

Telling Time

Numbers chalked clockwise inside the rim
Of the circle on the sidewalk,

The hands drawn upon it, *to* and *past*.

Time would change every time she erased
And realigned them, sectioning the face.

In hopscotch the numbers were boxed.

Now they were hours, the hands
At twelve folded shut like a fan,

Then spreading open till they closed again.

Such clockwork ticked through everything,
She told me, the seconds adding up—

Something that I should know,

Like my home address and whose number
To phone in an emergency.

Everything in sync with its own duration.

The miles-per-second at which light
Was clocked came years after that,

As did the time card I punched

At the start of each shift in the mills,
Feeding the furnaces a steady diet of days.

Eastern Standard, Daylight Savings Time . . .

A smudged clock on a sidewalk.
Time blown through the figures beside it.

Winter Nights Enlarge the Number of Their Hours

I.

Pittsburgh winter, the day closing up shop.
Small flakes falling into the privet hedges,
The streetlights burning in the dusk. Iron-
Cold rivers. Parked cars starred with frost.

The otherworldly beauty of the falling snow
As it blankets this one, the way it does
In black-and-white in movies from the '40s,
The clement soundstage heavens letting go.

II.

Slate skies. Flakes in a steady state. Grim winter the home movie
from 1993, our first full year in Regent Square. January 6th: 20
inches of snow, banks piled halfway up the meters, ruts gullying
the streets where the slush kept hardening into ice. January 19th:
22 degrees below zero, the city hypothermic, shutting down, that
one dull lamp burning amber in the alley behind the house, the
snow grown dingy with exhaust smoke and cinders. Then on
March 4th the fourth major storm of the season: a whiteout we
stacked along the warrens of the sidewalks, trenching our back-
and-forths. "I feel battered by this winter," someone said at the bar.
"Don't you feel battered by this winter?" Then later, as though in
response, someone telling the bartender, "I have a lot of drinking
I want to do tonight, don't try to put me in the weeds."

III.

Sfumato of hedges. The air with its cold iron edge.

Abbott Street

1993–1997

I.

Our flat paved length of latitude, Donny's Bar
At the far end of the block, East End Avenue
At the other, the Midwest on our doorstep.

II.

A dusting of snow last night, the neighbor's roof
Still ghostly at ten in the morning.

Then like in a negative: the chimney's pale shadow
Slanting alone across the slates.

III.

I'd have seen it from a second-floor window
In the big corner house we were settling into.
High-ceilinged rooms and wide bisecting staircase
That met you at the door. Period piece features
Like the cast-iron cover for the fireplace,
Its embossed doe and fawn, the push-button
Light switches disked with mother-of-pearl.
Period piece among the basement rafters
Where knob-and-tube wiring connected the dots.
Oak floors when we rolled back the carpets.

IV.

Morning, the sound of traffic like rain
On the pavements, buses surging into their surfs.

Then the random tantrum of a car alarm.
A passing jogger. Mail dropping through the slot.

V.

Our four-year residence in the 14th Ward,
Getting the hang of things. Four fall burials
For the fig tree in our neighbor's backyard garden.
Four springs in which its resurrection
Was among the first things that he'd attend.

Years among our corbelled wooden mantels
And built-in kitchen hutch. The French doors
To the dining room. The linen closet upstairs.
We left a version of our lives there—
The one in which all four of us are still alive.

Metaphysics

In sixth grade, making those crystal sets,
We were taught how broadcasts entered the air

And then the stratosphere beyond us, riding
The dispersing currents of the universe itself.

They stayed intact, part of the steady state
You could actually tap into,
                                        replaying

Whatever you happened to find out there,
Even waves of cosmic flotsam, drifting out of date.

And that "equal and opposite reaction"—
What was it, I wondered, that doubled back

This way?
                When my wife died it was vertigo
And those weeks through which I floundered,

Starting the day I looked out my window
And saw the rubble of clouds on the ground.

Timelines

The April woods: jack-in-the-pulpits
Above the creek,
Each with a hooded candle,

Blackness like a bog
With its steeping teas,
And this patch of small white flowers,

Stippled as the candy
I quaffed by the box,
Saturday afternoons at the movies.

Soon the seasonal snow
Of blossoms will float on the trees.
Sno-caps! that was the name

Of the candy. Back then
The trees all towered above me,
Movie-screen big,

Like the ones in *Vertigo*
The lovers stroll among,
Discovering that slab of Sequoia,

A crosscut section
Of concentric rings, the Pacific
The sheer drop beyond it.

I doubt I took home much
From the movie
Other than a kind of mood—

Dreamlike, suffusing—
That was mostly a matter
Of its saturated hues

And Bernard Herrmann's
Great score. The string-section
Lushness I get cravings for,

Bowed from maple and spruce.
"*Sequoia Sempervirens*,"
One of the lovers says,

"Always green, ever living."
Then the centuries in that time-
Lined slab hang as if in effigy.

Elegy for the Park Theater

Every Saturday we thronged in droves
To the Cinema Paradiso in Homestead Park
Where we'd be plunged into darkness
Beneath the beam of light figures rode
Onto the screen: Shane and Hondo
And the mantis-like invaders from Mars.
The several avatars of Tarzan. I sat alone
With others, outsized by what I saw.
Cartoons and previews. The feature films
We could sit through again if we wanted
Or leave where we came in, taking bits
Of action with us to restage all week,
Each of us taking a crack at playing hero.
When the movie house closed down
I was lost. When it opened again
In my dreams it showed nothing but
Foreign movies: lurid, shadowy, Grade-B
Noirs without subtitles or dubbing.
Even the posters dripped with menace.
Night after night the same bad dream
In which I wound up on the sidewalk,
Staring up at nightmare's latest marquee.
The King of the Jungle, where was he?
And the Hollywood back-lot badlands?
They turned the theater into a roller rink,
The latest craze to sweep the Fifties,
But did so cutting costs—rows of seats
Unbolted from a floor they left sloping,
As before, toward the proscenium
Down in front, out from under my feet.

III

All Hallows

Propriety's little redbrick house.
My stepmother insisted that my father
Have it built, on the hill above
The cemeteries where she wouldn't
Have to see the steel mills churning
Out smoke or suffer the streetlights
Burning in the middle of the day. 1952.
Which meant Korea and lots of flags
On the graves and lots of parades,
Including the one held on Halloween.
That first year I can't remember
If I was among the ghosts and goblins
Being paraded down Main Street
Or was taken instead from door to door
In our strange new neighborhood.
The second Truman Administration.
A newly formed family working out
Its notions of itself, which meant trying
On costumes as well—Mom and Dad
And who are you? What I remember
Is the dead of night and being in
The bathroom. Had too many sweets
Made me sick? A minor mystery,
Unlike the why in which that mask
Was hanging on the back of the door.
For there in the darkness before me
Was the red-horned head of the devil
Who'd been lying in wait, just like
They said he did, and though I'd said
My prayers about dying in my sleep,

I couldn't get by him to save my life.
Or escape those waiting midnights
When I'd change into furnace greens,
My battered orange hard hat,
And pass once more among the flames.

Joining the Congregation

Burners from the top of a chop-shopped stove,
Or so it looked like, the hot plate
On which my lunch was heating up:

A single-serving can of Manhattan clam chowder,
Which was new to me as well.

I'd watched the bartender's wristy flourish
As he tapped it into the saucepan,
The grill set on sizzle beside him,

Behind the kind of counter I'd sat at before
Only when ordering sodas or ice-cream floats.

Still, I'm in my element, perched on a stool
Beside my father and soaking up the exotica
Of labels and posters,

Brand names in their cursive, neon,
Bird-of-paradise hues.

A Black-owned bar named *Snow's*!
One of language's early delights, just blocks
Above the main gate of the mills.

I breathe in the tang of malt and tannin,
The briny, insistent smell of the clams.

We sit there together—whetted, expectant—
The way we do at the Communion rail.
"Drink this in remembrance," said the priest.

St. Joseph, Abscondus

He's gone missing from the only kind of heaven
We have left in Homestead—
                                        the plate-headed saint

Who stood sentinel above Saint Michael's
For decades, dozing on duty

Through the vast dismantling of the steel mills,
Then that of the congregation, the Iron Age

Giving way to the Silicon.
                                        The diocese has been
Cutting its losses since then, Saint Mary's

The first to close, her biblical picture windows sold
And her copper downspouts and gutters,

The basement now mosaicked with mold.
To which write-offs you can add Saint Michael's,

Its saint gone missing as though derelict
Or salvaged from the masthead of the wreckage.

Voice-Over

I live in Homestead with ghosts, a voice says
Out of the blue, the town coming into view
Below me on my walk, a voice more overheard
Than thought out loud, more audio and earbud.
Down to my right, the twelve brick chimneys
Which rose in a line from the soaking pits
Now loom in memento, the Monongahela River
Beyond them and the Homestead Grays Bridge.
The ghosts of the steel mills lapse-dissolved
Behind the mall, ghosts on the avenue sidewalks
Chockablock bodies across. Tugboats
And barges. The voice a kind of status report
Sent from one crimp in the brain to another,
The one offhand, the other caught off guard.

II.

Working turns we called it, one week following
Another in the mills, the shifts with their own
Time zones: eight to four, four to twelve,
Twelve to eight, and *graveyard*, lunch breaks
In the middle of the night. The shifts with
Their jet lags. I never got used to eating dinner
First thing in the morning, heading to work
At bedtime or in the ghostly light that gathered
On winter afternoons. Keeping the Sabbath
Was an early casualty of the spinning jenny,
Clocks that never stopped. *Turns* like falls,
Two out of three, and you lost out on everything
You'd punched in from, your portion
Of labor under the sun shifting to fit the gears.

41

III.

Those frayed-nerve mornings on the way to work,
My father would stop off for a bracer,
The ghost of his Uncle Andrew leading the way.
The men at shift's end pouring into the bars
Or standing in line in bakeries to pick up
Their daily bread, lights still burning on the river,
Wraiths through the downdrafts of smoke.
And so loud by the furnaces you had to shout
To make yourself heard. Loud in the clamor
Of the coal cars. Ghosts hung in the laundry
Behind the crowded wooden houses,
In the semaphore strung above the courtyards
Of the vanished wards. Flagship tenements.
Voices carried upwards by the winds.

IV.

Or a small still voice, like the one from within
The whirlwind. *I live in Homestead with ghosts.*
A kind of remark made in passing, a kind
Of listening in, one half of the conversation.
"A good talking to," they used to say, in one ear
And out the other. Those wind socks of smoke
From the chimneys said that men were working—
The sledge of the forge and fire being bellowed—
Casting sheds the size of tabernacles.
"In the sweat of thy face shalt thou eat bread."
Voiced, silent, bicameral chatter.
Now, below me, the roof of an old bowling alley,
The rain-guttered ruins of the lanes . . .
How suddenly, in Genesis, it all comes undone.

An End to the Marriage: My Stepmother Buys Twin Beds

How, years later, when I remember those beds
And my father's obvious displeasure,
Am I to believe she ever took him in her hand
And then into her, returning her petals to the stem?

Now the only thing within arm's reach
Is his nightstand, my dead mother's rosary
Stashed in the back of its drawer.

Billeted now on that thin celibate bed,
How could he have risen the next morning,
Or any of the ones after that,
Only to enter the world at Homestead
Where light from the river, our poor open sewer,
Had backed up again past Braddock?

How could she have sent him into such a day
Or I have slept so soundly, all those years,
Right down the hallway?

The Hall Mirror

for Andrew

The one my father hung on my bedroom door
Gave back the hallway and offered another,
Secret one: a quarter-inch world
Whose depths were all surface and doubled
And half-again as filled with light.
I thought about it all again today,
Mounting a mirror on my youngest son's door—
Sorting brackets, soaping the threads of screws—
How a pane of framed still waters
Now will hover on the hinges to his room,
Light falling into the prisms of the bevel,
The film of silvering at the back of the glass.
Father, because glass is conceived in fire,
The quick breath flashed through its crystals.

Home Movies

I.

"I'm in Pittsburgh and it's raining,"
The fighter claims in *Requiem for a Heavyweight*,

His face in the mirror of the vending machine

A stray cloud darkening its glass,
The corridor he's been led down,

Half-dead on his feet, dim with the wattage

Our sky's now had for days, white sun burning
In the overcast, another front on the way.

The film's period feel is weather as well—

That grainy, on-location wash of light
The cameras have been filtered to capture,

The city the background and character witness.

Days in a row now, monochrome with drizzle,
The world slogged down for the count.

II.

The severe unspoken savor she brought with her
To the table, family gatherings after grace,

Your plate filled, as always,

With whatever had passed through her hands—
The aunt who'd married wearing weeds,

A black-clad Bride of Christ.

Mantle, habit, scapular, guimpe . . .
It's no wonder we called them penguins

Though they were no joking matter,

Looming up to bear down upon you,
Clutching those biker-chain rosaries.

Or in 1958, in *Vertigo*, the rope of the bell,

The mission nun having sent one of the lovers
Over the edge, the other right up to it.

Monostiches

Mother and *matter* both from the Latin root *mater*,

*

The strung beads sibilant under the breath

*

Where each "Hail Mary" was said, my mother

*

Fingering contrition down its requisite decades

*

Till she was thumbing the patina once again

*

From that savior's abraded brass face, the rosary

*

A kind of abacus upon which the tallying

*

Squared the account. I take it out again today,

*

My only memento of her, who died days after

*

They cut us apart, wondering again how much

*

Her piddling sins added up to in the first place

*

And what traces, if any, she's left behind

*

Among the small, linked roses—oils from her skin

*

Or the head-of-a-pin garlands of wilted DNA—

*

What traces of her might be configured here

*

Among the laths of these asterisked lines?

*

Necklace. Umbilical. Sleaving of dark carved beads . . .

*

Words in their traces when what matters is the flesh.

Varieties of Religious Experience

1. ON LEARNING X. NOW LIVES IN AN ASHRAM

Our first date and she was wearing a pair
Of knee-high, green-gray, crushed-suede boots,
Light catching changes in the nap.

Stacked heels and slim shafts.
They kept me on my toes, as did the thought
Of watching her zipper them off.

Most likely they were long gone long before
She discovered nonattachment.
Why not do without what can't last anyhow?

Today I caught that scent of flesh, heat,
And nylons among the secretaries on the street.
All these years, I'm still clinging to things.

2. GUMDROP TREE

Two jagged, plastic, espaliered halves
The color of rain on the windows. Every year,
Come Easter, we'd snap them together

To array with a rainbow of gumdrops—
One more tree to add to the season,
Like the hardwoods of Maypole and Cross,

The ritual freight of their blossoms.
We unpacked an annual archetype
Without once having heard the term.

For us those buds were just an edible spectrum
Snatched from the ends of the branches
Till the tree was bare and wintry again.

3. AUTUMN PENTECOSTAL

Here on our hill we're home to doves
And the names of doves—*turtle, mourning, rain*—
And the soft, beige, dove-gray feathers.

The sudden burst from cover when flushed.
The off-glide of the coos—liquid, cooling—
When they're settled in the shade of the trees.

Because they were the first game birds
Of the season, we waited, late afternoons
In cornfields, to take them on the wing.

Savored their small, heart-shaped breasts
In our first autumn stews, pungency
Like the spirit's descending on the tongue.

4. BURNT OFFERINGS

Phil Schavone's father ate the pizzle
Of every deer he killed, or so Phil insisted,
Describing how they sizzled in the skillet.

The first, best, part of the animal,
As the old man would have it, famished,
Reaching for the vinegar and salt.

We never knew whether to believe
Any of this or not—the ceremonial totem-
Tribute to the life just taken, or the usual

Adolescent rot? The jokes about lead
And pencils, and behind them,
The old, dismembered, scattered gods.

5. THE SACRED AND THE PROFANE

In Homestead the High-Roller Lounge abuts
The Community of the Crucified One,
Tossed dice adjacent to that brambled brow.

I wonder what Sister Ann would make of that,
Who sent me home from catechism class
For having a deck of cards—*cast lots upon*

my vesture—her outrage chapter and verse.
She cast me in the parable because
The world was literally as written down.

My Protestant friends preferred a cross
As severe as a Mondrian. Even now, non-
Believing, I need more marrow than that.

Frances Perkins at the Homestead Post Office

Her tricornered hat's all but trademarked,
Her suit's well cut and suitably dark.

Patrician disguise for our one great
Secretary of Labor, the tireless tony agitator

With her firm, man-the-barricades touch.
In 1933 she's in Homestead, drumming up

Support for the newly established steel
Code, the nascent agencies of the New Deal.

The borough hall's packed, with hundreds
More locked out—"undesirable reds,"

According to the burgess who refuses
To admit them or permit her the use

Of the stairs in front. Nor is Frick Park's
Municipal block ordinanced for such talk,

Or so they're insisting when she sees
The post office and, thinking *federal property*,

Sets up shop in its safe haven.
(Clerks and customers, their startled faces,

My Uncle Arch looking up from his desk.)
The cops are fuming, as is the burgess,

But there's not much that they can do now,
Even though theirs is a company town.

How close she came, during her tenure,
To putting paid to such places forever.

Minimum wage, overtime, social security . . .
A storm of progress to the angel of history,

The debris of paradise scattered about
The aggrieved, beseeching crowds.

IV

Bildungsroman

I'll call it *Portrait of the Artist Weeping*,
A little one-act set in my mid-teens:

A school-night and I'm in bed, windows
In their frames like Rothko's

Slowly disclosing their shapes,
Light widening in the hallway

Behind my father. He knows the cause,
Or thinks so, of my muffled sobs—

Being cut from the swim team—
And has on hand his hard-knocks speech

About the setbacks in life
And not feeling sorry for yourself.

And for a while we're in a scene
Straight from some late-night movie

Where resolution leads to fade-out
And gumption in the very next shot.

Alone again, the fields of darkness
Returning, it's that I couldn't care less

About the swim team that scares me.
About the high school either, or nearly

Any of the consensus things everyone
I knew was pledged to. And if none

Of that mattered, or marked me,
What hive would I comb? What honey?

The Age of Innocence

At our high-school dances we'd gather on the stairs
Where we could furtively smoke and swear

And make those first fumbling attempts
To manage what none of us could have dreamt

Was awe.
         As evening deepened around us,
The first stars wheeling together across

The sky, we spoke of *feels* and *pieces*, the supple
Couplings of tongues. Inside, the school

Throbbed with recorded thunder (the Ronettes'
Sultry "Walking in the Rain") and the garish

Colors of the cellophaned spots.
                All evening
We hurried back beneath those lights, burning

To wade once more into the slow clenched laps
Of the waters in which we drenched each dance.

II.

Hip-hoppers I know are too young to remember
The "Wall of Sound," or the groups them-

Selves—the Crystals and Ronettes—singers
Who swayed like lean black flames in concert

Behind their mikes, the layered welling
Of the instruments topped by the belling

Chimes.
        Turntabled tonight: the brute repetitions
And numbing rhymes from the graduation

Party now underway halfway down the block.
Decibels like heavy machinery. *Bitch* and *fuck*

Thudding across the lawns.
                I catch the flash
Of handshakes, their elaborate dance,

The few girls huddled by the cars,
Streetlights above them and the first wheeling stars.

Park Elementary

From across the street the sallow, bluff-
Faced building looks the same as when
I went there, its windows cluttered
With cutouts the sun's begun to fade.
Once inside, however, sunlight slants
Into stairwells and hallways—
Standard archaeologies—that could be
Anywhere at all. In one of these rooms
We learned the flag salute. In another,
Musical chairs taught us that winning
Left no room for anyone else.

It was in fourth grade that someone
Set a tack on Joanne Patson's chair
And we giggled till she got to her feet.
Rumpled and slow, with a sweetness
The boys at least were blind to, she was
The *dunce* they taunted, the loser,
In the mocking test they gave her,
Of her own spelling bee. She'd lose again
The day that collie came bounding
Down the hallway, licking our faces,
Sending her thrashing with fright.

They coaxed her into the cloakroom's
Would-be refuge, then shoved in
The big eager dog. What did her frenzy
Mean to us then? Everyone could see
The dog was friendly—wasn't she,
As usual, just getting things wrong?

Wasn't that our answer, months later,
When she was no longer among us,
The last report cards being handed out,
Passing us further into the world
For which we were being schooled?

Summma Theologiae

1. VERBATIM

I.

The broken-record hectoring I grew up with:
You're in for a rude awakening
And *better stop that bellyaching.*

There was *mend your ways* and *rue the day,*
And, coming home after school,
I've got a bone to pick with you.

II.

Rue and *ache* and *bone*, each word bearing its Scots inflection, whetted
on the kirk of the stone my stepmother lived by, though *rude (Sc. a.)*—
"marked by unkind or severe treatment of persons, etc."—can also mean
"deficient in literary merit," for which the OED gives us this example: "The
Apostles used freely a rude version of the Old Testament" (1861 STANLEY
East. Ch. viii. [1869] 271). She would have approved of that, adding her
own addendum: *No place to escape the wrath of God except heaven, and
not, at times, even there.*

2. GENEALOGICAL

I.

The world turning on the word until they clicked.
As with the affinities, or that day in high school
When *The Ginger Man* (a Dell paperback, kelly green)
Stopped me cold in an aisle of Jay's Book Stall—

"Today a rare sun of spring." The fragment's freshet
Of perception a kind of ideogram, it would seem
To me years later, but even then it was pure presence,
Cleft of its verb, like Adam's given-named animals.

II.

In the middle of the Ellis Island century—prefix, suffix—
Gibb got shucked from Fitzgibbon, misnaming
The generations of that émigré Adam, Roberts in a row,
Down to me. Knowledge I came to belatedly, like sex,
Or how Pittsburgh was on the edge of the Midwest,

III.

"Count yourself lucky," she told me. "If your mother
Were still alive, you'd be going to parochial school."

IV.

Shanty the slur I heard most often in that house.

3. THE TERMS OF MY CONVERSION

I.

Summoned by the spirit that summer,
I slipped into the woods behind our house,
Gathering green fanning branches
For the makeshift altar I was fashioning
In the cellar—a cloth-draped box
Decked with candles and the leafy display
I was suddenly wild to worship.

II.

"Put those flames out," she shouted.
"Do you want to set the house on fire?"
Which promptly doused the ceremony,
But not that awakened, pagan sense of things
Which has stayed with me ever since,
The god in the Gnostic gospel vascular
And immanent as the one inside the tree.

III.

I was deep in the distractions of my teens
When the woods were sold, clear-cut
For one of those tract suburban cul-de-sacs,
Split-leveled and sectioned into lots.
It looked to me like a patch of skin
Shaved around an incision, raw and what
I'd now call *glairy*, the sutures all tied off.

Coal Stove

A smoldering furnace on a slab of slate,
It threw off heat like a fuel-rod
When stoked with our local anthracite,
Bricks stacked in a firewall behind it.

Scuttle and bin and the film of dust
It left about, sooty and industrial—
A whole new rigmarole to me,
Who till then had only burned wood.

I'd handled a coal shovel though,
At the bottom of a shaft in a steel mill,
Loading wheelbarrows full of scale
Shed from the furnaces above me.

All night they kept me at it beneath
A ceiling that kept me stooped, load
After load through a hole in the wall,
As though I'd been sent down a mine.

It was fire in the hole that night
We came home to find a glowing stove
Warping the air around it, though
I'd shut the vents when we left.

The only thing I could think to do
Was damper the fire with more fuel
For it, smothering the coal beneath
A banked new layer, which worked,

The metal ticking slowly to black.
For the rest of the winter it was ash
And cinders, but no more choruses
Of "Burning Down the House."

Vandals

1999

Because the woods behind us are all under-
Mined with the spalled rooms of pillars

From which coal's been freighted away,
We had thought that we were safe

From the bulldozers we're hearing this year,
The chainsaw's dental snarl,
                                    as they clear-

Cut the lush, parceled acres,
Hauling off truckloads of timber.

(There must be people for whom the trees
Are not a necessary mystery.)

Now we're front row, center for the aftermath:
Backyard carnage,
                          churned up tracks,

The ovals of those raw, weeping stumps
Left to rot in the ground like pumpkins.

2001

Not the ones massed at the gates, whose rude
Infusions kept civilization new,

But the ordinary, homegrown kind,
Spray-painting their memorized lines

And crudely glyphed graffiti—
                              a hopscotch
Of hasty slogans and signs, slashed circles

Overlaying FUBU and BOSS,
Swastikas littering the parking lot like spurs.

What tattoo-cluttered skinhead's work is this,
I wonder, scrawled in its aerosol hiss?

I drag my toe across the emblems,
One part Aryan, the other pentagramed

In a heavy-metal version of the occult.
White Pride.
              Its two-bit Kristallnacht.

Deer Season

In the parking lot by the cell-phone tower,
That ash pit of a body, field-dressed
And headless, which some poacher tried
His best to set on fire, the pelt poor kindling,
Even with the help of the accelerant.

II.

She'd not given her menses a second thought,
She said, till she was already in the woods
A good distance from her house
And heard the day's first urgent belling
From what seemed only moments away.
"I wanted to flee like Daphne into a tree!"

III.

In Dürer's great engraving—horse, forest,
The stippled flock of birds circling
That mountaintop castle—St. Eustace
Is shown at the moment of conversion,
Kneeling before the miraculous stag
With a crucifix on its forehead, the trees
Become the sacred grove above him
And his stymied pack of hunting hounds.

IV.

The sound of crashing in the nearby woods
And a pair of bucks comes tumbling out,
Their grappling-hook antlers entangled,
Skidding sideways onto the road.
Their snorting nostrils and clattery hooves.
Everything from the brains on back
Straining forward, hotwired by the rut.

V.

A deer asleep in the covert at the bottom
Of our yard, wreathed in the mist of its coat.
It was there first thing this morning,
My son told me, bedded among goldenrod
And pokeweed and the bare forked branches
That spread twisting from its head.

VI.

Driving backroads home from Black Lick
In November, the leaves all fallen,
A few flakes eddying on the late-day air.
And down in a swale of smoke-blue shadow
A pair of hunters dressing the deer
They'd hung from a tree in their yard.
Barn and farmhouse and corn crib,
The coppery burr of sunlight topping the ridge.
We might have just elected FDR.

VII.

Tonight I'm reading *Go Down, Moses* again,
Paging to my favorite passages—the one
Where Issac almost steps on that rattler,
And the earlier one in which the mystic deer
Comes "walking out of the very sound
of the horn which related its death."
The deer Sam Fathers calls "Grandfather."

Skinhead

Walking up the steep wooded road
From Homestead, I hear shouting
From below me. Someone on his cell phone,
It sounds like, yelling at someone else:
"How much further? How much further?"
Then nothing but silence, the hillside's
Resumptive hum. And right on its heels
That question, "How much further?"
Louder now and asked of me, I realize,
When he storms into sight—shaved head,
Shirtless, calligraphic with tattoos.
And so cranked full of amphetamines
He's careening wildly inside his skin.
"She's just called the cops," he blurts out,
"I'm fucked big time if they spot me."
A few more furious steps and he wants
To know, "Where's Union Street?"
As if he'd just this minute misplaced it.
I try explaining the address he wants
Is one hill over from the one we're on,
But it's impossible. "How many miles
Are there in a hundred yards, one or two?"
Then he starts pin-balling back and forth
Across the road, frantic with the bag
He's clutching, and sure he'll have
A heart-attack at any moment now,
Mounting his meth-induced mountain.
"There's the cops," he says, dropping
Into a crouch when an ordinary car
Drives past, as though his inked slogans
Don't still expose him. Then, once again,
He's back to "how much further?"

That heartsick, wits'-end, question.
"Union Street. Can you take me there?
I'd pay twenty bucks right now for a lift."
When the road divides I send him left
Into the subdivision whose mazy streets
Funnel into his and hurry on alone
Up the last steep stretch of the road.

From the top of the ridge I can hear him
Demanding answers down below—
"102 Union Street. Where's my house?"—
A stoned wraith cornered in the open,
Lost within shouting distance of home.

Skunk Journal

I.

The black-and-white part of the landscape,
He lumbers across the yard, thickly plumed,
Wedge-headed as the poet said, for whom
Skunks and their appetites were nightmare.

II.

Ravenous, he'll scarf up beetles and crickets,
Havoc beehives and the nests of ants,
Cramming his wet snout with fungi, mast,
The heady whiffs coming off of carrion.

III.

Making him the likely plunderer of my lawn,
Its moonstruck caller, clawing holes—
Those scattered spun-grass whorls
From which he's grubbed something up.

IV.

Squunk, out of the Proto-Algonquian—
*/sĕk-/ meaning "to urinate,"
*/-aːkw/ meaning "fox"—which translates
Into puckered nozzles, set on spray,

V.

And an adage: *even one skunk is a surfeit.*
The threat of whose stinging, rancid mists
All but predator-proofs it.
Even so, skunks prowl mostly at night.

VI.

So what's brought him out in the daytime?
That lumbering's begun to worry me
(Injury? Fermented berries? Rabies?),
Who gets thrown off balance so easily myself.

VII.

I'd barely begun this poem when a girl
Was shot on her way to a cousin's party. Dusk
And he somehow mistook her for a skunk:
Small, far-off, padding into consequence.

Century Elegies

Beginning with laments for that animal merit

Killed on the highways, whales on the wastes
Of the seas. For gray wolves shot from gunships.

The last woodland bison hunted to extinction

One New Year's Eve, the men marching down
From the Seven Mountains into the 19th century,

Their hymns on the darkness like a killing frost.

II.

When the next century was barely underway,

Firestorms howling in the blackened bells
Of the great Bessemer thuribles, my grandfather

Was killed in Homestead in the steel mills.

Elegies as well for the waters that caught fire
That night, for the arks of that country

In which all nature was now a resource for steel.

III.

Elegies for the hang-time implosions of the mills

At the close of the last century, salts of the metal
Bulldozed back into the earth, the great sheds

The wreckage of that La Brea, their ridge vents

Shattered like spines. Elegies for the mill floors
Left abandoned to the weather, their concrete

Seamed with fireweed, sumac's burning saps.

IV.

And for my half-orphaned father, who spent

His century's most eloquent hours listening
As if sitting in with Armstrong and Basie

And Homestead's Maxine Sullivan, who he knew.

LPs as well as 78s, the stylus riding rhythm
Through the grooves. Against the cold hymns

Of dominion: the sweet rebuttal of the blues.

NOTES

"The Pittsburgh Athletic Association": Oakland is a Pittsburgh neighborhood. The Carnegie Library of Homestead features a concert hall in its eastern wing and athletic club in its western.

"Musicology": The Blind Boys of Alabama's version of "House of the Rising Sun" can be found on their album *Spirit of the Century*.

"Last Round: For Rufus Harley": The quoted phrase at the end of the poem comes from Keats's "Lines Written in the Highlands."

"The Etymologies of Rust": The poem incorporates details from the *Oxford English Dictionary*.

"Interiors": The quoted line in "Coal Cellar" (from "The Play of Memory in Childhood Spaces") is, of course, from Robert Frost's great poem "After Apple-Picking."

"Frances Perkins at the Homestead Post Office": The angel of history and the debris of paradise are both from Walter Benjamin's *On the Concept of History*.

ACKNOWLEDGMENTS

Arts & Letters: "The Hall Mirror," "Deer Season"

Blueline: "Skunk Journal"

Brilliant Corners: "Musicology," "Impulse!," "Last Round: For Rufus Harley," "The Immanence of 78s," "On the Removal of the Stephen Foster Statue from Schenley Plaza in Pittsburgh"

The Ekphrastic Review: "*Homestead, ca.1929*. Oil on Canvas"

The Galway Review: "Joining the Congregation" (as "Confirmation Class"), "Phone Booths"

The Gettysburg Review: "The Pittsburgh Athletic Association"

Great River Review: "Metaphysics," "Vandals"

New Madrid: "Skinhead"

Notre Dame Review: "The Age of Innocence," "Verbatim" (from "Summa Theologiae"), "Varieties of Religious Experience" (as "Studies in Comparative Religion"), "Century Elegies"

Parhelion Literary Magazine: "All Hallows" (as "Trick or Treat")

Pittsburgh Quarterly: "Home Movies"

Poetry East: "Bildungsroman," "Pittsburghese"

Prairie Schooner: "St. Joseph, Abscondus," "Voice-Over," "The Terms of My Conversion" (from "Summa Theologiae")

Sou'wester: "Park Elementary"

Speckled Trout Review: "Monostiches" (as "The Sorrowful Mysteries"), "Coal Stove"

Stand: "Telling Time," "Winter Nights Enlarge the Number of Their Hours," "Elegy for the Park Theater"

Virginia Quarterly Review: "An End of the Marriage: My Stepmother Buys Twin Beds"

Vox Populi: "Deskulling the Slag Pots," "*Home Scrap Project: Unemployed Steel Worker, 1987–1988*," "*Worker, Steel Mill*," "Frances Perkins at the Homestead Post Office"

SERIES ACKNOWLEDGMENTS

We at Wheelbarrow Books have many people to thank without whom *Pittsburghese* would never be in your hands. We begin by thanking all those writers who submitted manuscripts to the thirteenth Wheelbarrow Books Prize for Poetry. We want to single out the finalists, Mary Ardery, Nancy Gomez, Jill McCabe Johnson, Moira Magneson, Clare McQuerry, Christine Rhein, SM Stubbs, and James K. Zimmerman, whose manuscripts moved and delighted us and which we passed onto the competition judge, Tyehimba Jess, for his final selection.

Our thanks to Kelsey Block, Jenny Crakes, Allyson Davidson, Claire Donohoe, Kseniya Lukiy, Estee Schlenner, and Jane Vincent Taylor for their careful reading of manuscripts and insightful commentary on their selections, and especially to Laurie Hollinger, assistant director at the RCAH Center for Poetry, who also read the manuscripts and provided the logistical aid and financial wizardry for this project.

We go on to thank Dylan Miner, dean of the Residential College in the Arts and Humanities, and former dean Stephen Esquith, who gave his initial support to the Center for Poetry and Wheelbarrow Books. Conversation with June Youatt, former provost at Michigan State University, was encouraging and former MSU press director Gabriel Dotto and former assistant director Julie Loehr were eager to support the efforts of poets to continue reaching an eager audience. Catherine Cocks, former interim director for MSU Press, gave us valuable advice and support as we worked through details of our contract. Thanks also to Lauren Russell, director of the RCAH Center for Poetry, for her support of Wheelbarrow Books. We cannot thank all of you enough for having the faith in us, and the love of literature, to collaborate on this project.

Thanks to our current editorial board, Sarah Bagby, Gabrielle Calvocoressi, Leila Chatti, Carol V. Davis, Mark Doty, George Ellenbogen, Carolyn Forche, Tyehimba Jess, George Ella Lyon, Thomas Lynch, and Naomi Shihab Nye for believing Wheelbarrow Books was a worthy undertaking and lending their support and their time to our success.

Finally, to our patrons: without your belief in the Wheelbarrow Books Series and your generous financial backing we would still be sitting around the conference table adding up our loose change. You are making it possible for poets, when publishing a new volume of poetry is becoming harder and harder these days with so many presses discontinuing their publishing of poetry, to find an outlet for their work. As well, you are supporting the efforts of established poets to continue to reach a large and grateful audience. We name you here with great admiration and appreciation:

Beth Alexander   Fred Kraft
Gayle Davis   Jean Kreuger
Mary Hayden   Brian Teppen
     Patricia and Robert Miller

There are many others whose smaller contributions we value whether those contributions come in terms of dollars, support for our programming, or promoting the books we have published and the writers we treasure. Thank you, one and all

WHEELBARROW BOOKS

Anita Skeen, *Series Editor*

Sarah Bagby   Carolyn Forché
Mark Doty   Thomas Lynch
George Ellenbogen   Naomi Shihab Nye

Wheelbarrow Books, established in 2016, is an imprint of the RCAH Center for Poetry at Michigan State University, published and distributed by MSU Press. The biannual Wheelbarrow Books Poetry Prize is awarded every year to one emerging poet who has not yet published a first book and to one established poet.

SERIES EDITOR: Anita Skeen, professor in the Residential College in the Arts and Humanities (RCAH) at Michigan State University, founder and past director of the RCAH Center for Poetry, director of the Creative Arts Festival at Ghost Ranch, and director of the Fall Writing Festival.

The RCAH Center for Poetry opened in the fall of 2007 to encourage the reading, writing, and discussion of poetry and to create an awareness of the place and power of poetry in our everyday lives. We think about this in a number of ways, including through readings, performances, community outreach, and workshops. We believe that poetry is and should be fun, accessible, and meaningful. We are building a poetry community in the Greater Lansing area and beyond. Our undertaking of the Wheelbarrow Books Poetry Series is one of the gestures we make to aid in connecting good writers and eager readers beyond our regional boundaries. Information about the RCAH Center for Poetry at MSU can be found at http://poetry.rcah.msu.edu and also at https://centerforpoetry.wordpress.com and on Facebook and Twitter (@CenterForPoetry).

The mission of the Residential College in the Arts and Humanities at Michigan State University is to weave together the passion, imagination, humor, and candor of the arts and humanities to promote individual well-being and the common good. Students, faculty, and community partners in the arts and humanities have the power to focus critical attention on the public issues we face and the opportunities we have to resolve them. The arts and humanities not only give us the pleasure of living in the moment but also the wisdom to make sound judgments and good choices.

The mission, then, is to see things as they are, to hear things as others may, to tell these stories as they should be told, and to contribute to the making of a better world. The Residential College in the Arts and Humanities is built on four cornerstones: world history, art and culture, ethics, and engaged learning. Together they define an open-minded public space within which students, faculty, staff, and community partners can explore today's common problems and create shared moral visions of the future. Discover more about the Residential College in the Arts and Humanities at Michigan State at http://rcah.msu.edu.